D0336309

STEP-UP
HISTORY

Viking Invaders and Settlers

Peter D. Riley

Evans

Published by Evans Brothers Limited
2A Portman Mansions
Chiltern Street
London W1U 6NR

© Evans Brothers Limited 2006

Produced for Evans Brothers Limited by
White-Thomson Publishing Ltd,
Bridgewater Business Centre,
210 High Street,
Lewes, East Sussex BN7 2NH

Printed in Hong Kong by New Era Printing Co. Ltd.

Project manager: Ruth Nason

Designer: Helen Nelson, Jet the Dog

Consultants: Rosie-Turner Bisset, Reader in
Education and Director of Learning and Teaching,
Faculty of Education, University of Middlesex;
John Haywood, Honorary Research Fellow in the
Department of History at Lancaster University.

British Library Cataloguing in Publication Data

Riley, Peter D.

Viking invaders and settlers - (Step-up history)
1. Vikings - Great Britain - Juvenile literature
2. Great Britain - History - To 1066 - Juvenile
literature
I. Title
942'.014

ISBN-10: 0 237 530392

13 - digit ISBN (from 1 Jan 2007)

978 0 237 53039 6

Picture acknowledgements:

Bridgeman Art Library: pages 15t, 21b, 22;
Camera Press: page 5; Corbis: pages 7t (Werner
Forman), 9t (Ted Spiegel), 9b (Ted Spiegel), 10t
(Archivo Iconografic, S. A.), 10b (Richard T. Nowitz),
13 (Ted Spiegel), 14 (WildCountry), 16b (Ted
Spiegel), 23 (Homer Sykes), 26b (Nik Wheeler),
27 (Macduff Everton); Mary Evans Picture Library:
page 6; John Haywood: page 19t; Science Photo
Library: page 26t; Topfoto: pages 4t, 25t, 25b;
York Archaeological Trust: cover and pages 4b, 7b,
12, 15b, 16t, 17, 18, 19b, 20t, 20b, 21t.

Maps and diagrams by Helen Nelson.

Contents

People on the move

There were Ice Ages in the past when most of the British Isles were covered in ice and it was impossible to survive there. About 10,000 years ago the last ice sheet melted and the countryside developed.

Stone Age migrants

Stone Age people moved to Britain from Europe. They lived by hunting animals and gathering fruits and nuts. In their homeland their numbers had been rising and there was not enough food for the larger population. People migrated to find food.

The first farmers

About 5,700 years ago a new kind of immigrant moved into Britain. These people were farmers. Their numbers had increased and they moved to find more land for growing food and rearing animals.

▶ *This timeline shows some examples of the remains left behind by people who lived in Britain in the past. Archaeologists examine the remains to find out about the people.*

c. 8000 BC

Ice sheet melts.

Stone Age people move in and live by hunting and gathering.

They use stone tools like these, which have been found at several places in Britain.

c. 3700 BC

People begin to farm in Britain.

c. 500 BC

People called Celts move to Britain from around the River Rhine.

This is the time of the Iron Age when people in Britain build hill forts. The remains of one can be seen at Maiden Castle, Dorset.

0 AD

This year is counted as the year of the birth of Jesus Christ. Dates are counted 'before Christ' (BC) and from the year of his birth (AD – *Anno Domini,* Latin for 'in the year of the Lord').

AD 43-410

Romans invade and conquer Britain, which becomes part of the Roman Empire. The Romans build Hadrian's Wall to keep out invaders from the north.

5th century AD

Anglo-Saxon tribes invade Britain.

AD 793

Viking raiders begin to attack Britain.

AD 865

Viking Great Army sweeps through England and Vikings settle in Britain. Many Viking remains have been discovered in York.

Celts, Romans and Anglo-Saxons

Two thousand five hundred years ago people called Celts arrived in Britain from their homelands around the River Rhine. They too emigrated because their population had increased.

Romans invaded Britain in AD 43. They came to conquer the land and eventually they made it part of the Roman Empire. Roman rule of Britain lasted for about 350 years, until AD 410. Many Roman soldiers were stationed in the country.

Soon after the end of Roman rule, Anglo-Saxon invaders arrived from Northern Europe. They took over the land and settled in it.

The arrival of the Vikings

Then, in 793, Viking raiders arrived on the British coast. They looted the places they attacked and took their booty home. Eventually the raids turned into an invasion and in 865 a large Viking army swept through England. Viking settlers moved in behind it to

▶ *Today some people interested in the Vikings take part in battles (without causing injuries!) to see what it was like when a Viking army invaded.*

set up home. In this book you can find out more about the Vikings who invaded and settled in Britain.

Continuing migration

Many more people have moved into Britain since then, from around the world. Do you know someone who has moved from another country to Britain, or perhaps from Britain to another country?

Who were the Vikings?

The Vikings were people who lived from the eighth to the twelfth centuries in the region of Europe that we now call Scandinavia. Late in the eighth century they began to travel away from their own lands. Some Vikings traded with people in other lands, while others raided places and carried off goods and people. They sold the people they captured as slaves.

An Anglo-Saxon view

One description of Vikings can be found in the Anglo-Saxon Chronicles. These were a record of events, year by year, written by a group of monks in Britain. The record starts from the year of the birth of Christ, but the monks only began writing at the end of the ninth century. For events until then, they used information from earlier documents. Then they began to record events as they happened. The last record was made in 1154.

▲ This picture of Viking raiders arriving at dawn is from a nineteenth-century history of Britain. How true-to-life do you think it is?

793 The ravaging of heathen men destroyed God's Church at Lindisfarne through brutal robbery and slaughter.

◀ This is a translation of the record for the year 793 in the Anglo-Saxon Chronicles. What impression does it give of the Viking raiders?

A fearsome picture

The Anglo-Saxon records of raids and battles led historians to think of the Vikings as violent people. Many pictures drawn in the nineteenth century show Viking warriors with horns on their helmets. This made them look fearsome. However, archaeologists showed that this was not accurate.

Archaeologists' findings

When archaeologists excavated sites of Viking settlements, they found helmets that did not have any trace of horns attached to them. Horns were found and you can read about their use on page 19. Many of the artefacts archaeologists discovered, such as a carved antler comb, showed that the Vikings took part in peaceful everyday activities.

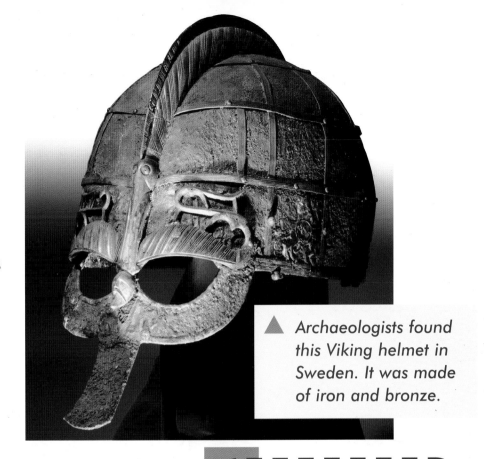

▲ Archaeologists found this Viking helmet in Sweden. It was made of iron and bronze.

◄ This comb was carved from an antler. What does it suggest about the person who owned it?

Examine your shoes

Archaeologists use artefacts to infer what people were like in the past. Shoes are artefacts. Look at your shoes. What do you think an archaeologist could infer from them about people in the 21st century?

The Viking homelands

Vikings lived in a region of Northern Europe that we call Scandinavia today. This region has long, cold winters and short, cool summers.

▼ *The Viking homelands in Scandinavia are Norway, Sweden and Denmark. Look at the coastlines of these countries. The small bays where many Vikings lived were called viks. This may have led to the name Vikings.*

Farming

The climate was not particularly good for farming, but the Vikings managed to grow crops and rear animals for food. In summer some Vikings would leave their farms and take their cattle and sheep up into meadows on the mountainsides. In winter the animals were kept in one end of the farmhouse. The heat from the animals helped to keep the inside of the farmhouse warm while the outside was covered in snow and ice. How do you think the inside of the farmhouse smelt in winter?

Fishing and hunting

The Vikings' homelands had long coastlines. People settled there and used boats to fish in the sea. The Vikings also hunted wild animals such as deer and bears for food. They used the animals' fur for clothing and for trade.

ICELAND

Arctic Circle

Atlantic Ocean

NORWAY

SWEDEN

FINLAND

IRELAND

North Sea

DENMARK

Baltic Sea

UNITED KINGDOM

0 100 200 300 400 500 600 miles

0 100 200 300 400 500 600 km

◀ Archaeologists have reconstructed Viking settlements, such as this village in Denmark, so that people today can imagine what it was like in the past.

▶ What artefacts do you think these archaeologists found at Hedeby, an important Viking trading place?

Trade

In Viking times much trade was carried out by exchanging goods. The Vikings traded furs, amber and walrus ivory for pottery and metals such as silver and gold.

Why did the Vikings emigrate?

Historians are not sure why Vikings began to move out of their homelands. Possibly their population grew so large that there was not enough farmland to provide food and they could not gather enough goods in their own lands for trade. The Vikings probably began raiding to gather goods for trade. Then, finding it easy to win battles, they started to take land too and settle in it.

Reasons for moving

Look at news reports of people on the move today, either as immigrants or as refugees. What are their reasons for moving? How do they compare with the reasons we believe the Vikings moved?

The Viking longship

We know about longships mainly from pictures and from archaeological finds. Pictures of Viking ships are provided by the Vikings themselves, as carvings on funerary stones in their homelands.

▶ *This picture on a funerary stone from Sweden shows the shape of the sail on a longship.*

Ship burials

Vikings were pagans. When Vikings died, they were buried with some of their possessions to help them in their life after death. Rich leaders of Viking groups owned longships and, when they died, a ship was buried with them. Some of these ship burials have been excavated and provide a great deal of information about how the ships were built.

◀ *This ship, called the Oseberg ship, was found in a burial mound in Norway. It would have carried about 40 Vikings.*

Ship design

Some longships were 25 metres long. In the centre was a vertical mast, which held up a horizontal pole called a spar. A woollen sail was hung from the spar and held in place with ropes attached to the hull. The hull was made from overlapping planks attached to a large piece of strong wood that made the keel. There were holes in the topmost planks of the hull, which were used to hold oars when the sail was not in use.

The longships were designed so that they could sail in shallow water and travel a long way upriver. But they could make long sea journeys too. The overlapping planks made the hull flexible so that it could bend a little in large ocean waves without breaking up.

▶ *Viking explorers used longships to sail to the Shetland islands, the Faeroe islands, Iceland, Greenland and even North America. They 'island hopped', building settlements on islands and using them to provide supplies for longer journeys to the West.*

Make a longship

Look at the picture of the longship and use it to mark out a longship shape 25 metres long and 3 metres wide. Try to arrange your class inside the shape like the crew on page 13 and imagine what it might have been like to sail across the sea in such a small ship.

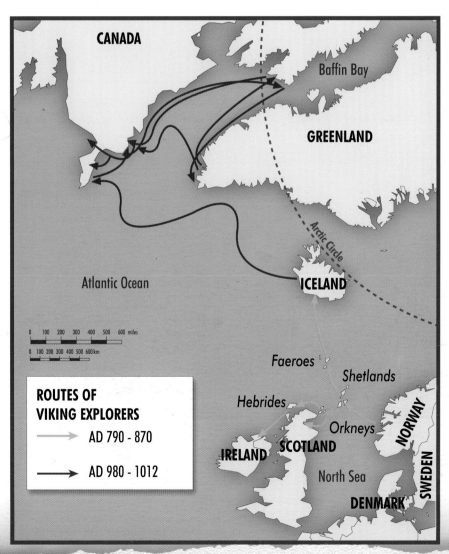

ROUTES OF VIKING EXPLORERS

→ AD 790 - 870

→ AD 980 - 1012

Viking raids

On the right are some records of Viking raids on Britain from the Anglo-Saxon Chronicles. In these records the Vikings are called:

- heathens or heathen men
- ship-companies
- ship force or force
- Danes.

From the records, make a list of the places where the battles took place and use an atlas and its index to find them on a map of Britain.

▼ This is a modern artist's reconstruction of a Viking battle.

793 The ravaging of heathen men destroyed God's Church at Lindisfarne through brutal robbery and slaughter.

794 The heathens in Northumbria ravaged and robbed Ecgfriths monastery at Jarrow. There some of the war leaders were killed; also some of the ships were broken up in bad weather, and many drowned. Some came alive to shore and were quickly killed in the river's mouth.

835 Heathen men ravaged Sheppey.

836 King Ecbryht fought with twenty-five ship-companies at Carhampton and there was great slaughter. The Danes held the battlefield.

838 A great ship force came to Cornwall.

840 Ealdorman Wulfheard fought at Southampton against thirty-five ship-companies, made great slaughter and took the victory...ealdorman Aethelhun fought with the Danes at Portland, with the men of Dorset; this ealdorman was killed, and the Danes held the battlefield.

841 Ealdorman Herebryht was killed by heathen men, and many of the people of Romney Marsh with him. That year again, in Lindsey, East Anglia and Kent, many men were killed by the force.

843 King Aethelwulf fought at Carhampton against the companies of thirty-five ships, and the Danes had the power of the battlefield.

▲ The Vikings were not always successful. In 840 an Anglo-Saxon noble, Ealdorman Wulfheard, defeated the Vikings. In which year did the weather contribute to the failure of the raid?

Viking beliefs

The Vikings worshipped a god of war called Odin and considered it an honour to fight in battle. Their swords were very important to them and they gave them names such as 'leg biter'. If a warrior was injured, he would probably die from his wounds. The Vikings believed that if a warrior died bravely, servants of Odin called Valkyries rode over the battlefield and took his soul away to be with Odin.

Method of attack

To increase their chance of winning a battle, Vikings tried to take their enemies by surprise. As they approached land, they took down the sail of their longship so it could not be seen. They used oars to row quietly up a river, then collected their swords, shields and axes and left the ship. They used loud cries to scare away their enemies. If their enemies ran away, the Vikings could take what they wanted without injury and stay fit to fight another battle.

Viking weapons

Make card models of Viking weapons, using their actual sizes. A sword had a blade 80cm long and 6cm wide, with a handle 20cm long and 3cm wide. A shield was circular, 1m in diameter. For an axe blade, follow the diagram. The axe handle should be 1m long and 4cm wide.

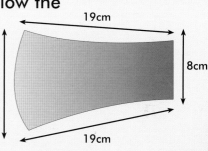

19cm

12cm

8cm

19cm

In this reconstruction of a Viking ship, you can see how the oars were held in holes in the hull.

Why did the Vikings raid monasteries?

Monasteries were centres of the Christian religion in Anglo-Saxon Britain. Some of the first monasteries were in the north of Britain. For example, Iona was built on a small island off the west coast of the Isle of Mull. Lindisfarne was built on Holy Island, off the east coast of Northumberland. Jarrow was built by the River Tyne in Northumberland.

▼ *Monasteries were often built in remote places where the monks could worship quietly. The monastery on Iona was raided by Vikings in 795. The church there today was built at a later time.*

Precious objects

Christian services of worship took place in monasteries and the monks had a range of objects to use in these services, including crosses, goblets to hold wine and dishes to hold bread. Worshippers at the monastery gave money so that the objects could be made of the finest materials, such as gold and silver, to honour God.

A monk's life

Imagine you were a monk living quietly on the island of Iona. Suddenly the alarm is sounded. The Vikings are coming! How would you feel about this?

At Iona, the captains of trading ships called in to ask for a blessing for their journey. They gave the monastery grain and wine. At other monasteries grain was also gathered in and stored. The grain was used for food for the monks and to feed the poor and any travellers who passed by.

Part of the monks' work was to copy holy books. To show their importance the books were bound in leather covers decorated with jewels and held shut with silver clasps.

When Vikings attacked the monasteries, they discovered all their treasures and stole them to trade in their homelands.

Peaceful monks

A monk's life was one of peace. Monks spent their time in worship, working on their farm and books, and caring for the poor. They were no match for Viking raiders and did little to resist them. Some monks ran away. Others who stayed to confront the Vikings were either killed or taken prisoner and sold as slaves.

When Vikings found holy books like this one, they ripped off the jewels and precious metals for trade. The pages were burnt, thrown away or stuffed into wet boots to dry them after the Viking raiders had waded ashore.

This carving on Holy Island shows Vikings taking part in a raid.

15

From raiders to settlers

A raider makes a surprise attack on a place and then goes away. The Vikings who first visited Britain were raiders. But in 865 a large army of Vikings arrived in East Anglia and set up camp. This army was known as the 'great heathen force', but we shall call it the Great Army. Use a map of Britain to trace its path.

Vikings used horses to travel to a battle, but always fought on foot.

The Great Army takes control

Soldiers from the Great Army attacked areas around their camp in East Anglia and stole food and horses. After a year the Army moved north and captured York. Anglo-Saxons there took five months to form an army, which attacked the Great Army and lost. The Vikings burnt villages and crops around York and took control of the area.

People who enter a country fully armed and take control of it are called invaders. The Vikings had changed from raiders to invaders.

The invasion continued the following year when the Great Army marched to Nottingham. People there did not fight but made peace with the Vikings. In 870 the Great Army returned to East Anglia and, as they took control of the area, King Edmund of East Anglia was killed.

This wall painting in a church represents King Edmund being killed by the Vikings. The artist painted the Vikings dressed in clothes from his own time, not from Viking times.

The arrival of Viking settlers

Gradually, northern, eastern and southern Britain came under the Great Army's control. More Vikings then arrived from Scandinavia to set up permanent home in Britain. They were not warriors but craftsmen and farmers and their families. They were settlers.

Some set up home in towns that the Great Army had captured. York was made the capital of the region of Britain that the Vikings controlled.

Find the settlements

York, Derby, Nottingham, Leicester, Lincoln and Stamford were all Viking towns. Find them on a map of England. Also find the mouth of the River Trent, near Hull. The Trent is an example of a river that the Vikings used as a 'highway' for transporting people and goods.

Viking remains in York

Archaeologists found many Viking remains in York, which helped them to discover what life was like in Viking times. Viking objects survived in York because the soil was unusual, lacking oxygen. Microbes rot down objects in the soil if oxygen is present.

▼ *Viking remains in York were uncovered when a factory was pulled down. Archaeologists excavated the site for five years. Now a shopping centre and the Jorvik Centre Viking museum have been built there.*

Viking life

Archaeologists have excavated Viking settlements and used their findings to help us understand how the Vikings lived. One settlement that has been excavated is at Jarlshof in the Shetland islands, but the most information has been found from the excavations in York.

Archaeologists working there have collected over 40,000 objects from Viking times. Some, such as quern stones used for grinding corn, were carefully dug out of the ground. But tiny objects, such as seeds from a Viking toilet, were removed from the soil by sieving.

The seeds were identified by comparing them with seeds of fruits growing today. The seeds from the toilet showed what kinds of fruits the Vikings ate.

Identifying seeds

Collect seeds from different fruits that you eat. Put some of each kind in separate clear plastic bags and label them. This is your reference collection. Mix the others in a bucket of sand, then sieve the sand to find the seeds. Can you identify each seed you find from your reference collection?

From the study of all the objects found, a section of the Viking settlement at York was recreated. You may be able to visit it at the Jorvik Centre.

◀ *Visitors to Jorvik travel in electronic cars through reconstructions of Viking streets, like this one with its market stalls selling leather and pottery.*

Houses

Vikings used local materials to make their homes. Houses in York had walls made from wooden planks and a thatched roof made from reeds. Inside was a hearth where a fire burned to keep the home warm and provide heat for cooking. A hole in the roof above the fire let smoke escape.

Beds were placed along the walls of the house. There was also an open space for a loom, used for weaving cloth for clothing.

▲ In the Shetland islands Vikings built their houses from stone. These are the remains of Viking houses in Jarlshof.

◄ Houses had just one large room with a fire in the middle of it. In this reconstruction at Jorvik you can also see some quern stones.

Food and drink

The Vikings stored food in pots, but some fish or meat was hung from the roof. Many kinds of meat were eaten, including chicken, goose, pork and venison. Vikings living near the coast collected gull eggs to eat.

Vikings made hearth cakes from barley flakes, oatmeal, butter and salt and heated them slowly in a pan. They used horns as cups to drink wine or beer.

Viking crafts

The Vikings were great craftspeople. They used a variety of materials to make the objects they needed and often decorated them in pleasing artistic styles.

Blacksmiths

Probably the most important craftsman was the blacksmith. He had a forge for heating iron until it was soft enough to shape. The hot soft metal was removed from the forge and shaped by placing it on an anvil and hitting it many times with a hammer. This needed great strength.

The blacksmith made many items that the Vikings needed for their survival – from swords and axes to spoons and needles. He also made tools such as clippers and chisels that were used for other crafts.

Leatherworkers

The leatherworker used awls and needles made by the blacksmith. Leather is a tough material made from

▲ *See if you can identify these items made by the blacksmith. What might they have been used for?*

cattle hides. An awl was used to make holes in leather and a needle was used to stitch pieces of leather together to make shoes. Beeswax was used to coat the needle so that it could slip easily through the small holes and speed up the stitching process.

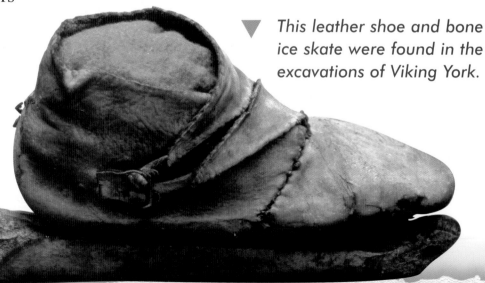

▼ *This leather shoe and bone ice skate were found in the excavations of Viking York.*

Woodworkers

The woodworker used axes to chop wood into pieces that he could cut and shape with chisels. Some woodworkers used a lathe to spin a piece of wood as they shaped it with a chisel.

▶ *Wooden bowls and cups were made on a lathe. The wood was made to spin by moving the foot at the bottom of the rope.*

Bone and antlers

Viking craftspeople worked with two materials that we do not use today – bone and antlers. These materials were carved into handles for knives and other tools. They were also used to make pins and finger rings. Bones were used to make the runners on ice skates, while antlers were used to make combs (see page 7).

▶ *Chess pieces carved from walrus ivory were found buried in sand dunes in the Hebrides. The skill of the carver is shown in the detail, such as the eyes and the folds in the clothes.*

Carve a chess piece

Use a plastic knife to carve a piece of Plasticine into a chess piece like the one in the photograph. Does your skill match that of a Viking craftworker?

The Viking language

The Vikings spoke a language called Old Norse. It is similar to the Icelandic language that is spoken today.

Sagas

The Vikings did not keep written records like the Anglo-Saxon Chronicles. They made long stories about their history, which storytellers learned by heart and passed from one generation to the next. The stories were called sagas. We know of them today because, from the thirteenth century, some people living in Iceland, who could write, listened to the stories and wrote them down.

What can the sagas tell us?

A saga told the story of a famous Viking who had performed a heroic deed. The sagas are thought to be a mixture of fact and fiction. The fiction was added to make the story more exciting. However the facts provide evidence of how Vikings lived. For example, in Njal's saga there are descriptions of clothing. A man is described in a blue tunic, blue striped trousers and black boots, while a woman wore a blue cloak and a scarlet skirt. Both wore silver belts.

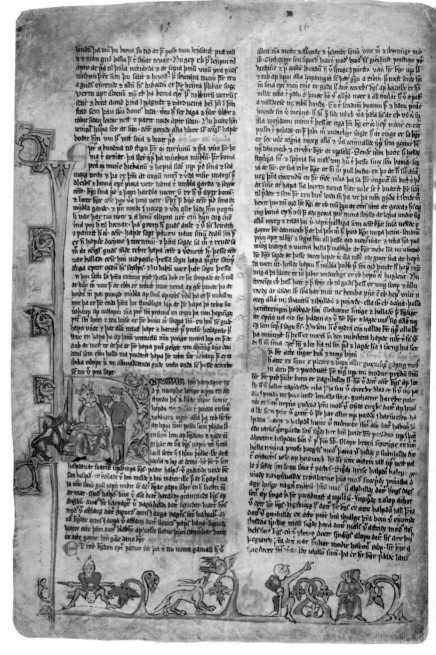

▲ Manuscripts of the Viking sagas are a valuable source of information about life in Viking times. This page is from a saga that was written down in the fourteenth century.

Writing

The Vikings did have a system of writing. The letters, called runes, were made by straight lines. This made them easier to cut in the Vikings' writing materials of wood, bone or stone than letters with curves in like some in our alphabet.

The Vikings used writing to show that they owned certain objects, just as you may write your name inside a book or on your pencil case. They also used writing to tell people about themselves or their family, by making carvings on stones such as funerary stones.

▶ *The alphabet of runes is called the futhark, after the way the first six runes were pronounced.*

◀ *Viking runes on a stone in the Orkney islands.*

A message in runes

Write a message in runes to a friend and see if they can translate it.

Runes	like our letter	pronounced as in
ᚠ	f	fog
ᚢ	u	cool
ᚦ	th	thick
ᚨ	a	ball
ᚱ	r	red
ᚲ	k and c	kite, cake
ᚷ	g	go
ᚹ	w and v	win, vote
ᚻ	h	hat
ᚾ	n	needle
ᛁ	i	deep
ᛃ	j and y	jam, yellow
ᛇ	ei	ride
ᛈ	p	pin
ᛉ	z and final r	zigzag, car
ᛊ	s	sun
ᛏ	t	top
ᛒ	b	big
ᛖ	e	day
ᛗ	m	man
ᛚ	l	long
ᛜ	ng	ring
ᛞ	d and th	do, then
ᛟ	o	pole

King Alfred and the Danes

The area of Britain that was settled by the Vikings was called the Danelaw. In this area people followed Viking customs and obeyed Viking laws.

While Viking settlers moved into the Danelaw, Viking warriors fought battles to make it larger. They attacked regions ruled by Anglo-Saxons. The largest of these regions was the kingdom of Wessex. It was ruled by King Alfred from 871 until his death in 899.

Alfred's battles with the Vikings

Alfred's first battle with the Vikings occurred only a month after he was crowned king. His army was defeated. However, the Vikings did not take over Wessex because Alfred paid them a large sum of money to leave his kingdom alone.

Over the next five years Alfred built up a strong army and navy. The Vikings could see that his power was increasing, and so they made a surprise attack and almost captured him. Alfred fled to the protection of some marshland and spent several months there making plans for a battle with the Vikings.

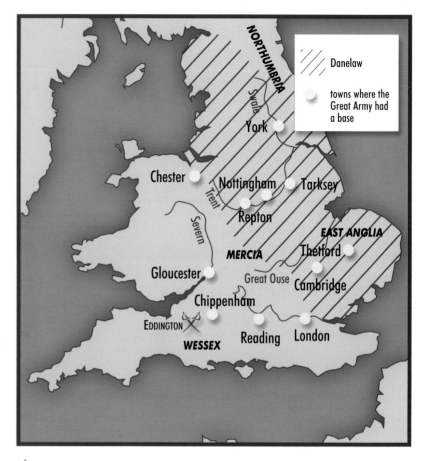

▲ The Anglo-Saxon regions of Northumbria and East Anglia were part of the Danelaw, but Wessex remained in the control of King Alfred. Which region do you live in?

A tale is told that during this time a herdswoman asked Alfred to watch over some barley cakes as they baked by the fire. He was so busy with his plans that he forgot about the cakes and they were burnt.

Alfred's plans were successful and in May 878 he defeated Guthrum, the Viking leader, at the battle of Eddington. The Vikings agreed that they would no longer try to take more land for the Danelaw.

Alfred was not satisfied with this and gradually he won back land from the Danelaw. In 886 he took London from the Vikings and set the western boundary of the Danelaw. It was the Roman road called Watling Street, between London and Chester.

► *Alfred is the only English king to be called 'the Great'. How does this statue give the impression that he was a great man?*

What makes a leader?

Discuss these features with your friends: a good fighter, good at winning arguments, handsome or beautiful, a loud voice, clever, kind, fair, likeable. Think of other features to add and discuss them.

▲ *Alfred's picture is included inside the letter 'A' in a manuscript recording the laws he made. These laws were eventually applied to the whole of England. Alfred also enjoyed learning and encouraged his people to become better educated by following his example.*

Thinking about the Vikings

Violent?

If you told someone that you had been studying the Vikings, they would probably reply, 'Oh they were violent, weren't they?' Try it. Written evidence such as the Anglo-Saxon Chronicles and artefacts such as swords and shields show that the Vikings did go into battle and were brutal victors. But what qualities do you think the Vikings should be remembered for?

Practical

The Vikings were certainly practical people. They managed to farm in some inhospitable regions, built strong ocean-going ships and were skilled craftsmen.

Brave

The Vikings were also brave. They set off on voyages across the North Atlantic to discover new lands and explore them. In many places they used their practical skills to create new settlements.

▲ Spacecraft sent to the planet Mars in the twentieth century were called Viking 1 and Viking 2. Perhaps you can find some other examples of the name 'Viking' being used for modern things. What qualities do you think the name 'Viking' suggests to people today?

◄ This statue in Iceland shows Leif Eriksson, a Viking explorer who was the first to reach America.

Fair

In settled regions, such as the Danelaw, the Vikings made laws for the people to obey. In Iceland they set up a meeting called the Althing where all the people discussed their concerns and expressed their differences of opinion, in order to improve the way the country was run. Historians consider that the Althing was the first parliament in the world.

▼ *This is a view of the 'parliament plains' at Thingvellir in Iceland. This is where meetings of the Althing took place, to decide peacefully how the country should be run.*

Vikings and Anglo-Saxons

Viking settlers in the Danelaw mixed with Anglo-Saxons who did not move out of the area. Vikings and Anglo-Saxons traded together and Viking words became added to the English language so that both sets of people could understand each other better. Some people consider that every seventh word we speak today is a word with a Viking origin. Here are some examples: big, build, crash, gaze, hurry, lift, odd, rinse, shiver, sniff, talk and wag.

▶ *Names of Viking settlements had the endings –by (farm or village), –toft (site of a home), –thorpe (hamlet) and –thwaite (a clearing or meadow). Find examples on a map of Britain. Where on the map will you look?*

ALLERTHORPE

Viking words

These English words have a Viking origin. Use each one of them in a sentence to show that you know its meaning: blunt, doze, fidget, grab, jumble, nab, swagger, whirl.

Glossary

amber	a yellow-orange, see-through fossil resin from coniferous trees. It is used to make jewellery.
Anglo-Saxon Chronicles	documents in which records of events from 1 to 1154 AD were written down by monks living in Anglo-Saxon times.
antler	one of a pair of bony branches that grow from the head of some deer.
anvil	a flat-topped metal block with one pointed end, used by a blacksmith when shaping hot metal.
archaeologists	people who study history by excavating sites inhabited by people in the past.
artefact	an object made by humans for a particular use or as a work of art.
awl	tool with a small point, used to make holes in material such as leather.
axe	tool used for chopping wood and bones and also used as a weapon.
blacksmith	person who shapes hot metal by beating it with a hammer while it is held on an anvil.
blessing	statement made by a priest in which God is asked to protect someone.
booty	property collected by theft in a raid.
brutal	cruel and savage.
chisel	tool used for carving wood or stone.
Christ	the name Christians give to Jesus, who they believe is the Son of God.
Christian	a person who believes that Jesus was the Son of God, sent to live on Earth.
Dane	a word used by Anglo-Saxons for the Vikings. It also means people of Denmark.
Danelaw	an area of England occupied by Danish Vikings.
emigrate	to move out of a country to live elsewhere.
empire	a large area of land, which may comprise many countries, ruled by one people.
excavate	to dig a hole in the ground.
forge	a very hot fire raised off the ground in which metal is melted or softened before being used by a blacksmith.
funerary stone	a carved stone put up to commemorate the life of a person who has died.
futhark	the alphabet used by the Vikings.
grain	the single seeded fruit of a cereal such as wheat or barley.
hearth	the place where a fire is set up inside a house.
heathen	a word used in the past to describe a person who was considered by others to have no religion such as Christianity.
hides	the skins of animals such as cattle which are made into leather.
immigrant	a person who moves into a country in order to settle there.
infer	to deduce or make a decision about, from things that can be observed.

inhospitable	unwelcoming. An inhospitable place has conditions which threaten the survival of people trying to live there.	population	the people who live in a certain place such as a town or a country.
invade	to enter a country with the intention of conquering it.	quern stones	specially shaped stones for grinding up corn to make it into flour.
ivory	a white material made from the tusks of elephants, walrus and a whale called the narwhal.	raiders	people who make a rapid attack on others and take them by surprise.
Jorvik Centre	a place in York where a Viking settlement has been recreated.	ravaging	destroying everything in a wide area.
lathe	a device on which a piece of wood is spun while it is being carved.	reconstruct	to make a model representing what something might have been like.
loom	a device for weaving cloth.	refugees	people who move to an area to escape from danger.
loot	to steal.	runes	letters in the Viking alphabet.
marshland	wet ground with reeds and pools.	sagas	long stories which tell the deeds of Viking heroes.
microbe	a tiny living thing that can only be seen by using a microscope.	Scandinavia	an area of northern Europe including Norway, Denmark and Sweden.
migrate	to move from one area to another.	service	a sequence of prayers, readings and music dedicated to God.
monastery	a place where monks live and worship.	settle	to stop moving around and stay in one place.
monks	men who live under strict religious rules such as taking part in acts of worship several times each day.	settlement	a place where people have settled to live.
oxygen	a gas in the atmosphere which is needed by living things for a process called respiration.	sieving	a process in which large and small particles are separated using a wire mesh.
pagans	a general term used for people who follow a religion which is not one of the major world religions. Some pagans worship rocks, trees and springs.	site	a place where an archaeological investigation is made.
		slaughter	the killing of many people at once.
		soul	the part of a person that many people believe lives on after the body dies.
		venison	the meat of deer.
parliament	a group of people who have the power to make laws to rule a country.	warrior	person with skills in using weapons and prepared to fight in a war.

For teachers and parents

This book is designed to support and extend the learning objectives for unit 6C of the QCA History Scheme of Work.

The ancestors of the Vikings settled in Denmark, Norway and Sweden hundreds of years before the people that we call the Vikings emerged. These Viking ancestors were farmers, fishermen and hunters. The Vikings also had these skills but in the period about 800–1100 (the Viking times) they developed another skill – the building of large, fast, ocean-going ships called longships. They used these ships for trade but when they discovered how easy it was to use them for raiding, attacks on Britain began.

Our knowledge of the Vikings comes from a variety of sources which cover the area travelled by the Vikings from North America to Eastern Europe. The remains of settlements have been discovered in North America, Greenland, Iceland and Northern Europe. At these sites large amounts of artefacts have been found, ranging from weapons and ships to coins and jewellery. The Vikings had an alphabet but wrote little. They preferred an oral tradition of passing on stories (called sagas) and information. The sagas were eventually written down in the thirteenth century and even though they contain some fantasy they also give an insight into the Viking way of life.

After many years of raiding Britain the Vikings became settlers. They eventually ruled a large area of England called the Danelaw and in 1016 a Viking called Cnut (or Canute) became King of England and Norway. After Cnut died his sons ruled for a short time but the English crown eventually returned to the Anglo-Saxons when Edward the Confessor became king in 1042. When Edward died the right to the crown of his successor, Harold Godwinson, was contested by the Viking Harold Hadrada, King of Norway. In early 1066 Hadrada and Harold fought in battle just outside York at Stamford Bridge and Hadrada was killed. This marked the end of Viking times in England.

Studying the Vikings provides an opportunity to develop children's historical skills, particularly in understanding the range of sources of information available and making inferences from evidence. There are opportunities for cross-curricular work, particularly in literacy, mathematics and design and technology. In the following list of activities there are suggestions to support children's work in ICT.

SUGGESTED FURTHER ACTIVITIES

Pages 4 – 5 People on the move
Although the focus of this book is the raiding and settling of Vikings in England, the children may gain a wider view of the Vikings' travels with this activity. They should use an atlas to find these places that the Vikings visited: Istanbul (Turkey) – for trade; Paris (France), Pisa (Italy), Seville (Spain) – targets for raids; Dublin, Limerick, Waterford, Wexford, Wicklow (Ireland) – settlements; Reykjavik (Iceland) – settlement; near Narssaq (Greenland) – settlement; L'Anse-aux-Meadows (Newfoundland) – temporary settlement.

Pages 6 – 7 Who were the Vikings?
For the 'Examine your shoes' activity, you could give the children some headings to use such as: materials, how pieces are joined together, the shape of the shoe, the size of the shoe, the condition of the shoe (signs of wear).
The children could follow up the section on archaeologists' findings by visiting http://www.yorkarchaeology.co.uk/secrets/anglescan.htm and selecting buttons in the Viking section on the left of the screen.

Pages 8 – 9 The Viking homelands
The Vikings made long journeys to trade, especially into Eastern Europe. When a deal had been made, for example to sell an item for a certain weight of silver, the trader produced a hand-held set of scales, put a weight on one pan and asked the buyer to add silver to the other pan until the two pans balanced. The children could make a simple balance scale with a ruler and two card discs (the pans) of about 6cm diameter. These could be suspended from each end of the ruler by three pieces of string and sticky tape. A piece of Plasticine the size of a pea could be put on one 'pan' and silver paper put on the other until the scales balance. This would help reinforce the notion that the Vikings did have a civilised aspect to their way of life.

Pages 10 – 11 The Viking longship
The children can find out a wealth of information about longships at http://www.cdli.ca/CITE/vikingships.htm. They could select a ship and make a report on it for a presentation in class.

Pages 12 – 13 Viking raids
A timeline which shows raids and journeys of exploration over the Viking period can be seen at http://www.viking.no/e/etimeline.htm. The children can compare the activities of the Vikings in England with their activities elsewhere.

Pages 14 – 15 Why did the Vikings raid monasteries?
To help them imagine life as a monk, the children could try this activity. Monks kept silent for much of the time so that they could focus their thoughts on God. At meal times Bible readings were made and the monks remained silent. They evolved a series of signs to ask for the things they needed. For example, rubbing one finger over another

meant 'I would like a knife', spreading the fingers and then lowering one hand meant 'I would like a cup'. Challenge the children to invent some signs to help them have a meal in silence. Then try it.

Pages 16 – 17 From invaders to settlers

On pages 6-7 the idea that Vikings wore helmets with horns when they went into battle was shown to be wrong. It seems true that Vikings wore helmets in battle, but what did they wear in peaceful times as settlers? The following activity can be used, with younger children, to set the scene for considering Vikings in peace time and also to lead into further activities on Viking costume. The children should take a piece of paper or card and make a circle with a diameter of 18cm. A segment of 45 degrees should be cut from the circle and the two edges of the segment pulled together and stuck with paper to make a cone. This shallow cone, made of wool, was worn as a cap by boys. The boys in the class could try it. The children can find out more about Viking costume at http://www.viking.no/e/life/eclothes.htm.

Pages 18 – 19 Viking life

The children could place some grains of oat, barley or wheat (from a healthfood store) between two small flat stones (about 10cm x 8cm) and rub one stone over the other to grind the grains. They can assess their skill at making flour but must not use it to make food.

Pages 20 – 21 Viking crafts

The crafts described on these pages needed considerable physical strength and would most likely have been carried out by men. Weaving and spinning are crafts in which women would have been involved and children could do some research into this. They could also consider how the spinning process produces a strong material. In the spinning process fibres become twisted round each other to make a thread called a yarn. The children could try to make a very simple yarn by pulling out a piece of cotton wool and rolling it between the finger and thumb. This can then be pulled further and rolled again. The drop spindle used by women for spinning in Viking times can be seen at http://www.regia.org/like/textiles.htm.

Pages 22 – 23 The Viking language

Some Vikings erected a stone by a road to tell people about themselves or their families. Sometimes they carved a body of a snake on the stone and wrote a message in runes in it. The children could paint a cereal packet pale brown or grey to represent a stone, then draw a snake with a body about 3cm wide around one side. They could then write a message in the body of the snake.

Pages 24 – 25 King Alfred and the Danes

To build on the introduction of the Anglo-Saxon Chronicles on pages 6 and 12, the children could read a translation of the Anglo-Saxon Chronicles which describes Alfred's battles with the Vikings: http://www.britannia.com/history/docs/asintro2.html (starting at 871).

Pages 26 – 27 Thinking about the Vikings

Vikings used to meet together to settle disputes. The meeting was called a *Thing*. To give the children an idea of how it worked, ask them to work out a dispute in Viking life: e.g. a shipbuilder is using so much wood that there is little left for the other villagers to use as fuel on their fires to warm their homes and cook their food. Two groups – one representing the shipbuilders' family and the other representing the villagers – prepare and then present their case to a third group who decide what should be done.

ADDITIONAL RESOURCES

Websites

http://viking.hgo.se/Files/VikHeri/Viking_Age/homelands.html (a short, straightforward account of the Viking homelands for children).

http://www.viking.no/e/england/york/jorvik_british_trade_routes_m.html (shows possible Viking trading routes through Britain from Jorvik).

http://www.viking.no/e/england/york/map_jorvik_trade_abroad.html (shows the possible Viking trading routes from Jorvik [York] to other countries. It can be used with the website above to show that Vikings were a trading nation).

http://www.viking.no/e/england/york/jorvik_trading_centre_5.html (a quiz about Viking trade, including a map for children to download).

Books and videos

English Heritage, *Viking Age England*, by Julian D. Richards (Batsford) provides a wealth of background information for adults.

Curriculum Bank History 1 (Scholastic) has lesson plans on Vikings with differentiation, assessment activities and photocopiable worksheets.

Viking raiders and settlers (Atlantic Europe Co Ltd) has a student book and teacher's guide, supported by a picture poster pack and integrated website (available at www.Curriculum Visions.com).

A video on Vikings suitable for 7-9 year-olds is available from http://www.bbcschoolshop.com.

Other children's books about the Vikings are published by Evans Publishing in their *Stories from Ancient Civilisations* and *Gods and Goddesses* series.

Role play activities in a Viking camp

A full day programme of role play activities called the Viking Experience is available to schools at The Environment Education Centre, Penwortham, Lancashire. For further details, email: Email@penwortham.cix.co.uk or telephone: 01772 751110.

The Young Archaeologists' Club

The magazine of the Young Archaeologists' Club has up-to-date information on archaeological digs, competitions and quizzes. YAC members can take part in archaeological activities at branches around the country. Contact: The Young Archaeologists' Club, Bowes Morrell House, 111 Walmgate, York YO1 9WA. Telephone: 01904 671417. Email: yac@britarch.ac.uk   Website: www.britarch.ac.uk/yac

Index